the
NEW KIND *of* LOVE

E. W. KENYON

the
NEW KIND
of
LOVE

GOD'S HEART CRY TO
BROKEN HUMANITY

WHITAKER
HOUSE

Unless otherwise indicated, all Scripture quotations are taken from the American Standard Version of the Holy Bible. Scripture quotations marked (YLT) are taken from *Young's Literal Translation* by Robert Young (1898). Scripture quotations marked (KJV) are taken from the King James Version of the Holy Bible. Scripture quotations marked (WEY) are taken from *The New Testament in Modern Speech: An Idiomatic Translation into Everyday English from the Text of "The Resultant Greek Testament"* by R. F. (Richard Francis) Weymouth. Scripture quotations marked (MOFF) are taken from *The Bible: James Moffatt Translation*, © 1922, 1924, 1925, 1926, 1935 by HarperCollins San Francisco; © 1950, 1952, 1953, 1954 by James A. R. Moffatt.

The New Kind of Love
God's Heart Cry to Broken Humanity

Kenyon's Gospel Publishing Society
P.O. Box 973
Lynnwood, WA 98046-0973
www.kenyons.org

ISBN: 978-1-64123-953-0

Printed in Colombia
© 2023 by Kenyon's Gospel Publishing Society

Whitaker House
1030 Hunt Valley Circle
New Kensington, PA 15068
www.whitakerhouse.com

Library of Congress Control Number: 2022950315

1 2 3 4 5 6 7 8 9 10 11 ⨎ 30 29 28 27 26 25 24 23

CONTENTS

THE AUTHOR'S REASON

We are passing through the most critical period of human history. All that has been built through the centuries is in danger of being destroyed.

Is there a remedy that can be applied at this dark hour that will save the situation?

Our home life is disintegrating. The whole moral structure of family life is endangered.

There is something lacking. Natural human love has failed. Again and again, we have asked the question, "Why has it failed?"

It is because it is based upon selfishness. It has been unable to stand the tremendous test of selfishness that has been developed by modern education.

There is a combat that is touching every life. It is the war between natural human love and selfishness, and love is losing the fight. You see it in the divorce court, in the struggle between capital and labor, between the classes.

Has God a solution for this problem? We believe He has.

It is *The New Kind of Love* that has been overlooked by the church, but has recently been rediscovered. This book is an attempt to bring this new kind of love into the modern life.

HOW IT CAME

For years, I had the conviction that I did not understand love. I knew Jesus majored it, and it was majored in the Pauline revelation. I gave much time to the study of it, but I always had the sense of not having arrived.

One day, I saw an article by Canon Frederic W. Farrar in which he called attention to the fact that there were two Greek words translated as "love" or "charity" in the New Testament: *agape* and *phileo*. He said that agape was evidently born in the realm of divine revelation, for that word did not occur in the classical Greek before the time of Christ.

Like a flash, I saw the truth. Jesus had brought a new kind of love to the world.

I saw that these two words are never used interchangeably. I had the secret.

John tells us that God is agape.

We partake of God's nature, eternal life, and this makes us sons of love.

1

LOVE, GREATEST THING IN THE WORLD

Love has never given birth to a pain. Love has never wantonly crushed or broken the tender flower of faith that grows in the heart of trust.

Love is God unveiled. *"God is love"* (1 John 4:8).

This love life is God actually living Himself in us as He lived in Jesus.

There was a ruggedness about the Master and yet a gentle tenderness that caused children to climb up into His arms and put their hands on His face. They longed to touch Him, to hold His hand, to be near Him.

The love that was in the Man of Galilee is the love that is to rule the church, rule the home, and rule this heart of mine.

Love is to the human heart what flowers are to the hillside. Flowers cover the naked, ragged places in the soil. They grow around the rocks. They grow among the roots. They cover up the wounds in the earth's surface. They cover the clay and bleak soil with a garment of glory, royalty, and lustrous beauty. So love covers the ragged rough spots in the human.

Love is the reason for the flower garden, just as love was the reason for the flowers being.

Love gathers the flowers and arranges them to please the eye and make glad the heart.

Love makes the home beautiful. Love comes and lives in the home to keep it a place of happiness.

Love is the most beautiful thing. It may be the most fragile thing, yet it has the most enduring strength of anything that we know.

When man is love ruled, love owned, and love motivated, he does not shrink from any sacrifice. Christ did not shrink from bearing the sin, pain, and anguish of the world.

LOVE AND THE CROSS

Love made that ugly cross beautiful. Love made that tomb beautiful—that darksome, dreaded place where death held sway. Love stripped death of its terror. Love made the naked, thorn-crowned Man of Galilee the King of lonely hearts.

My heart calls Him the naked King of the storm-tossed, broken human. Love made me crown Him, not with thorns, but with my heart and its devotion.

Love drives that delicate tender spirit into the darkest heathenism of Africa to endure every privation, to be shut alone with heathen minds that have no sense of appreciation, no touch of love, just cold indifference and selfish greed. And yet that love spirit lives, thrives, and pours itself out until that dark place blossoms with all the tender fragrance of the new creation.

Such is love, the mightiest thing among the mighty, and the most beautiful thing among the beautiful. It is this God nature gaining the ascendancy in the heart of man.

"EVEN AS"

There are two little words in the new law of the new covenant that challenged me. They reached out their tender hands and gripped me. I saw the dainty tendril of a climbing vine lay its soft, fragile hand upon the coarse, hard rock, and after a bit, it had fastened itself to the rock.

Those two little words seem like the delicate fingers of that beautiful climbing vine.

You ask me what the words are? *"Even as."*

This is my commandment, that ye love one another, **even as** *I have loved you.* (John 15:12)

At first, I tried to get away from them, but they followed me, followed as only love can follow. I could hear them in the chambers of my soul, like the memory of a long-forgotten hymn that comes back and raps at the door of the heart.

I kept saying, "Even as." Then I turned and listened. I asked, "Even as what?"

"As I have loved you."

I said, "I can't do it, Master. I can't love like that. If I loved like that, I would be obliged to give away everything I own."

Then He asked so gently, "What is it that you would need to give away?"

I took an inventory of the things that I felt I would have to give away if I loved *"even as"* He loved me.

After the inventory, I said, "But what would I get in place of these rich treasures of mine?"

Then He showed me wealth that I had never seen before. If I loved *"even as"* He loved, I would have His companionship. I would have His strength. I would have His gentleness and His forbearance. I would give away the toys of the senses to get the wealth of the Spirit.

LOVE'S METHOD

I would give away things that perish after much use to receive something that increased when used. I saw then a joy I had never known.

I had been seeking happiness. I did not realize that happiness came from things, people, and circumstances, that I could lose happiness as I once lost my knife. I saw what an illusion it had been.

I felt that I was willing to forego some of the things that make men happy, if I could have this joy.

This new life gives a joy that springs from love. Happiness springs from sensuous things around me. I found that joy was as far superior to happiness as the diamond is to glass, as gold is to common dirt.

Then I knew what love meant. I am to love even as He loved. I am to take His place.

He is seated yonder upon the throne, ministering to me, enabling me to take His place down here. I am to speak His words and to do the kind deeds that He would do.

I will feel the same kind of passion for the lost and broken that He felt.

I am to love in His place.

Oh, the joy, the unspeakable joy that comes. I have joy even as He had joy because I am loving even as He loved.

2

THE PLACE OF LOVE IN LIFE

It is hard to speak of love without becoming lyrical, without the spirit of poetry gaining the mastery.

We find ourselves in love's own realm of melody. We feel the pulsation of another world where hatred has never been. We feel the lift of a strange power that almost makes us float above the turmoil of bitterness, greed, and hatred.

Love is the reason for man's being. Man would not have not been created had love not been hungry ages on ages ago. Love brought men into being.

When man was created, the earth was full of music and laughter. Flowers abounded everywhere. Their perfume filled the air, and all creation sang its anthem of welcome.

Man had come! Love had conquered. Love had won.

LOVE TO BE THE LAW OF HIS BEING

Love is the healing for every wound. It is God's love poured upon the sore of human failure.

Love is the creative force in creation. It is the creative law.

Love is the reason for parenthood in every realm of life. Love brings fatherhood and motherhood into the holy union of expectation. Love waits for its offspring.

Love alone can give and nurture babyhood. Giving birth to a baby born outside of love is a crime against the child. Every child has a right to be love-born!

There is no crime among all the crimes in the realm of wrong like the murder of love. Love has given us all that is beautiful. When love is slain, all that is beautiful lies dead.

Love is the heart force of life. It is the homemaking force. If we go where there is no love, we will find no home. We may find a house and we may find furniture, but as soon as we enter the building, we are conscious of something lacking. We feel as though there has been a funeral or there is going to be one. It is dead love. It is unburied love. There may be wealth, but it is not a home.

Love and love alone has given us the sacred place called "home."

They do not have it in heathen lands where plural marriages are practiced. They have no home. It is just a habitation. Eternal life destroys polygamy.

A home is a thing born out of the Jesus kind of love. Love is the mating law of life. There isn't anything as utterly beautiful as the mating time. All creation celebrates it.

I saw a couple of doves celebrating the mating season. I saw the sparrows making love to each other. I saw the bees carrying the pollen from flower to flower. All creation mates, and all creation loves.

LOVE GIVES

I saw the blossom loving and giving itself to the fruit that was soon to take its place. I smelled the fragrance on the air as the rose gave its best to make others glad. I saw its beautiful petals turn brown and seared. I watched them as they dropped upon the ground. I saw the rosebush stand, dry and dead.

Why? It was love pouring out itself for others.

Love is the reason for life. When love is gone, life has lost its reason.

Love is the reason for all that goes to make civilization. When love dies, all worthwhile in life fades.

When love grows cold, the sun ceases to shine. The clouds gather, dark and ominous. The storm threatens. And we hide away in the darkness under the doom of lost love.

No wonder that broken fellowship has the deepest sorrow, the keenest anguish known to the human heart! No wonder that love flows at flood-tide when fellowship is the richest!

The heart is the life of man. Love is the life of the heart.

Love makes a romance out of the commonplace. It makes the ugly, lovely. It has a light of its own. It sheds a radiance over life that no sorrow can slay or destroy.

Love will redeem a wasted life and transform it into beauty and usefulness.

Love is a spiritual thing. It is above reason. It is not in the reason realm. It is God, invading the realm of the human.

RELATION OF LOVE TO ANSWERED PRAYER

The love walk is the love way. The love life is the way of the new covenant. When we step out of love, we step out of the will of the Master. Whenever we act out of love, we act contrary to the will of our Lord.

When our prayers are not answered, we invariably ask this question, "Have I stepped out of love?"

First John shows why prayer is often unanswered:

Hereby know we love, because he laid down his life for us: and we ought to lay down our lives for the brethren. But whoso hath the world's goods, and beholdeth his brother in need, and shutteth up his compassion from him, how doth the love of God abide in him?...Hereby shall we know that we are of the truth, and shall assure our heart before him: because if our heart condemn us,

God is greater than our heart, and knoweth all things.

(1 John 3:16–17, 19–20)

He knew when we turned our brother down and refused to help him that our hearts were not in sympathy with him. The Father knows when we close up our hearts of compassion.

He says, "*If our heart condemn us not, we have boldness toward God; and whatsoever we ask we receive of him, because we keep his commandments and do the things that are pleasing in his sight. And this is his commandment, that we should believe in the name of his Son Jesus Christ, and love one another*" (1 John 3:21–23).

Our refusal to help our brother was not pleasing in His sight.

The name of Jesus gives us access to the Father. But if we step out of love, the name is of no value to us. We can only use the name of Jesus as we walk in love. When we step out of love, it breaks our fellowship with the Father, weakens our faith, and makes the Bible almost a closed book to our hearts.

Love is the greatest thing in the world. It is the nature of the Father revealed to us.

The new law of the new family is that we love one another even as He loved us. (See John 13:34.)

If we are sick and do not get our healing, we should find out if we are walking in love.

Most people when they are sick become very selfish. This is not true in all cases, but it is in many cases. They have the whole family looking after them, ministering to them. Their selfishness takes them out of the love realm where prayer is answered.

If someone can pray for us and get our healing, we will not maintain it unless we walk in love.

We cannot love with words only. We must love in reality. That means bearing each other's burdens.

3

WHAT JESUS SAID

Jesus came to fulfill the first covenant with its priesthood, atonement, sacrifices, and law, and at the same time to establish a new covenant based upon a perfect redemption instead of atonement, giving to a new creation a new priesthood with new sacrifices and a new law. He says:

> *A new commandment I give unto you, that ye love one another; even as I have loved you, that ye also love one another. By this shall all men know that ye are my disciples, if ye have love one to another.* (John 13:34–35)

He gives us in this Scripture the new word *agape*, which is translated as either "love" or "charity."

Not only that, but based upon His finished work, He is introducing a new creation that is going to live under the dominion of this new law.

Stephen, in his defense in Acts 7:8, calls the first covenant *"the covenant of circumcision"* given to Abraham.

But the one Jesus is establishing is the covenant of the new creation. It is a circumcision of the heart prophesied by Ezekiel.

> *A new heart also will I give you, and a new spirit will I put within you; and I will take away the stony heart out of your flesh,*

and I will give you a heart of flesh. And I will put my Spirit
within you, and cause you to walk in my statutes, and ye shall
keep mine ordinances, and do them.   (Ezekiel 36:26–27)

This is a prophecy of the new creation of a recreated human spirit.
"*A new spirit will I put within you; and I will take away the stony heart*
out of your flesh." That is the heart of selfishness of the natural man.

"*I will put my Spirit within you.*" The new creation is going to have
the Holy Spirit.

Ezekiel 11:19 develops the thought a little further: "*And I will*
give them one heart, and I will put a new spirit within you; and I will
take the stony heart out of their flesh, and will give them a heart of flesh."

With one heart, they are all ruled by love. With a new spirit, the
old human spirit, the real man, is to be recreated with the nature and
life of God.

Again he says, "*And I will take the stony heart out of their flesh, and*
will give them a heart of flesh." This is the new covenant man.

The Jew entered the old covenant by circumcision. We enter the
new covenant by the new birth. The old covenant made them servants. The new covenant makes them sons.

In whom ye were also circumcised with a circumcision not made
with hands, in the putting off of the body of the flesh.
                                                    (Colossians 2:11)

The Spirit's argument is easy to understand. Our circumcision is
not physical but spiritual. It is God taking away not a portion of the
physical body, but putting off the body of the senses or flesh. That
means He is taking away the dominion of the physical body over the
human spirit.

When man was created, his spirit dominated him, but when he
sinned, the physical body gained the ascendency, and his spirit was
dominated by the body.

Here, Paul calls it "*putting off of the body of the flesh.*"

He tells us in Romans 6:6: *"Knowing this, that our old man was crucified with him, that the body of sin might be done away, that so we should no longer be in bondage to sin."*

Here the Spirit is trying to make clear in the language of the senses the fact that when a man is recreated, the physical body loses its dominion.

If we should put it in another way, in Adam, the physical body gained the ascendency in the fall. In the new creation, through Christ, the spirit wins back the ascendency over the physical body or the senses.

The reason why men could not love God and love one another under the first covenant was because the heart was selfish, dominated by spiritual death. The only love that he had was *phileo*, a love based upon selfishness.

Now we are prepared to understand what Jesus meant when He said, *"A new commandment I give unto you, that ye love one another even as I have loved you"* (John 13:34).

The natural man cannot do this, only the new creation man. You can see the absurdity of telling the world folk that they must love. They cannot do so until they receive the nature of love in the new birth.

> *Even as the Father hath loved me, I also have loved you: abide ye in my love. If ye keep my commandments, ye shall abide in my love; even as I have kept my Father's commandments, and abide in his love.*　　　　　(John 15:9–10)

The word *abide* here comes from the Greek word *meno*. It means "to settle down" or "to remain."

Jesus said, "I want you to settle down in My love just as I have settled down in My Father's love. I have remained in My Father's love. I want you to remain in My love."

In other words this new kind of love has created a new realm, a new kingdom. We are to settle down in that kingdom as permanent inhabitants, never to move out of the realm of love.

One ceases to be dangerous to others when he moves into the realm of love. Every migration out of the realm of love is into a land of danger.

Love becomes beautiful and very attractive as we continue to abide in love and let love abide in us.

This Scripture helps us to grasp it more fully:

And we know and have believed the love which God hath in us. God is love; and he that abideth in love abideth in God, and God abideth in him. (1 John 4:16)

I wish we knew what that meant in reality, in daily life, to have faith in love, greater faith than we have in any other law of life, for us to consciously know that we are living in the love realm, that we are acting as citizens should act who live in that realm, that we are taking our place as sons of love in the realm of love.

I am convinced that we would have to learn the love language, the love etiquette, and the laws that govern that wonder kingdom.

4

JESUS CONTRASTS THE TWO KINDS OF LOVE

JOHN 21

We all remember that beautiful scene in John 21 that took place after the resurrection of the Master. It was a cold morning. The disciples had been fishing all night and had caught nothing.

Cold and hungry, they started to row to the shore. As they drew near, they saw a man cooking over a fire.

He said to them, "*'Children, have ye aught to eat?' They answered him, 'No'*" (verse 5).

And he said unto them, Cast the net on the right side of the boat, and ye shall find. They cast therefore, and now they were not able to draw it for the multitude of fishes. (John 21:6)

John whispered, "It is the Lord."

When Peter heard that it was the Lord, he put his coat about him, cast himself into the sea, and waded to the shore. The disciples saw fish cooking on a fire and some bread.

Of all the pictures that we have of the Master, there is nothing as intriguing as this.

Jesus—who governed the universe with His Word, had just gone through the awful suffering of His substitutionary work, and was about to take His place at the right hand of the Majesty on High—steps aside for a moment and cooks breakfast for those cold, hungry disciples.

That is not the reason for His appearing, however. He wanted to give us this vivid contrast of the two words translated "love" or "charity."

"So when they had broken their fast, Jesus saith to Simon Peter, Simon, son of John, lovest thou me more than these?" (John 21:15). Jesus used the word *agape*.

Peter answered back, *"Yea, Lord; thou knowest that I love thee."* Peter used the word *phileo*.

A second time, Jesus asks, using the word *agape*, and again, Peter replies that he loves Jesus using the word *phileo*.

Then He asked Peter a third time, *"Lovest thou me?"* (verse 17). This time, the Lord came down to Peter's level by using the word *phileo*, the same word Peter used.

Peter was grieved. *"Lord, thou knowest all things; thou knowest that I love thee."*

Twice the Lord had used that new word *agape*. It is evident that the disciples knew about this word that Jesus evidently had coined because there was no question asked about it.

The Master unveiled to us the contrast of natural human love and the new kind of love that was to displace it after the day of Pentecost.

For years, I was confused about this love fact. One day, I discovered it in one of Canon Frederic W. Farrar's books. He said there are two Greek words translated "love" or "charity," and one of them is *agape*. It is not found in classical Greek before the time of Jesus.

Farrar says it is evident that the word *agape* was coined in the realm of divine revelation. That would mean that Jesus coined the word.

True, it is used several times in the *Septuagint* translation of the Hebrew into Greek, which was translated two hundred and eighty years before Christ. The only copies that we have today are those that were copied three to five hundred years after Christ. The word *agape* had then become current in religious literature.

5

THIS JESUS KIND OF LOVE

The measure of our love is the measure of our worth to society. Perhaps we have never thought of it in these terms.

Men are valued according to their financial or political standing in a community. It is a problem of how much money they have or how much political influence they can swing. Yet, in the final analysis, the men who love are the men who help the community.

Man was created by love to answer the heart cry of the Father God. Man outside of love is a failure.

Selfishness is the blighting curse of the human. Love stops the rust of selfishness, preserves the home and church life from decay. The lover is like rust-free steel. We know that the largest part of steel is destroyed by rust. We know that the largest portion of home life in America is destroyed by selfishness.

Marriage is wrecked by selfishness. The home life disintegrates because the husband is selfish, and the wife seeks her own. The children are born and grow up in that atmosphere. They go out into life handicapped.

It is a well-known fact that children who grow up in godly homes have a better chance in life than those who grow up in homes where there is quarreling and bitterness.

More than seventy-five percent of the boys and girls who are delinquent have come out of broken homes. It is almost impossible to find in any of our penal institutions a young man or woman whose father and mother were both walking in the new kind of love when the child was born and while it was growing up.

Love is God's adhesive power that binds us together.

LOVE MAKES THE HOME

I wonder if you have ever realized that the word *home* does not occur in any primitive language.

In the Bible, the word we have translated *home* comes from the Hebrew meaning "house," "tent," or "a dwelling place." It may be a place where a man lives with one or two or three wives. It is not a home.

The same thing is true of the Greek word that we have translated "home" in the New Testament.

"Home" in a Christian sense is the place where a man and a woman who have received eternal life, the nature of God, live in harmony. Men and women who have received eternal life never seek a divorce. You cannot find in the United States or Canada a case where a couple who have received eternal life and walked in love ever went to the divorce court.

Isn't that a staggering fact? Doesn't it show that there is a solution for the home problem and for marriage?

Selfishness separates, but *agape* binds together.

The new kind of love that Jesus brought to the world, which was manifested in His life first and then unveiled in the new church that came into being on the day of Pentecost, was God's solution of the home problem.

LOVE IS THE FRUIT OF THE RECREATED HUMAN SPIRIT

It took me a long time to make the discovery that love does not spring from our reasoning faculties. They never give birth to a love life. Love is born of the spirit.

The love of God hath been shed abroad in our hearts through the Holy Spirit.   (Romans 5:5)

The word *heart* is another term for *spirit*. These words are used synonymously.

After we are born again, we breathe into our spirits His love life just as we breathe air into our lungs.

There is no limit to the Jesus kind of love. It is of God. It is having God's nature within us. As we learn to give love freedom to develop, it will unveil to us the ability of God to help men.

We can train ourselves so that at the first dawn of consciousness in the morning, we will say, "I have God inside of me today. It is going to be easy to do my work because He is going to move through me today, act through me, love through me, and speak through me. I will not be left alone to meet any crisis. He will be there to make me a success."

Just as the vine drives its life into the branches, so does God pour Himself into us as we open our spirits to Him.

Knowledge has its limitations, but love knows none. How that thrills the heart! When we realize this fact, life becomes such a big, real, rich romance.

So every morning as you awaken, you may say, "Today, I am walking in love. Today, I am fearless. I have God's ability. I have God's nature. I have His love life."

Love is God in action. There is no love without action. God so loved that He gave. God so loved that He acted. Jesus so loved that He acted.

It would be a great day in your life if you would let love loose in you. It will mean letting God loose in you. His grace then would be without limitation.

Grace is love in manifestation.

We are bound to give thanks to God always for you, brethren, even as it is meet, for that your faith groweth exceedingly, and the love of each one of you all toward one another aboundeth.

(2 Thessalonians 1:3)

Think of abounding love among the brethren and love gaining the mastery in a church.

6

WHAT IT WILL DO

A man sat listening to our broadcast on love one morning and said to his wife, "I don't know what would happen in our office if I should practice this love of which he is speaking."

His wife said, "Why don't you try it, dear?"

He said, "I believe I am a coward."

She quickly quoted 1 John 4:18: "Perfect love casts out fear."

"Yes," he said, "I know that. You pray for me that I will have courage to begin to live this thing, because it is the biggest thing in the world."

A few days later, the wife said to her husband, "Dear, have you been practicing this Jesus kind of love?"

He said, "Do you know, it amazed me today. One of the men said to me, 'What has come over you? You are so different.'"

The Jesus kind of love had been manifested in this man. Love will transform your office and your home. It will make life different.

How sweet life becomes when we let love loose in us, when our hearts remember that Jesus loves us, even as the Father loves Him, and the Father loves us even as He loves the Master.

That the world may know that thou didst send me, and lovedst them, even as thou lovedst me. (John 17:23)

If the Father loves us as He loves Christ, He will never leave us. He will watch over us as a mother watches over her baby, but with infinitely more wisdom.

Let us say now, "Father, I thank You for Your love for me. I am going out and love even as Jesus and You have loved me."

THE LOVE SLAVE

In Romans 1:1, there is a startling Scripture when we understand it. *"Paul, a servant of Jesus Christ, called to be an apostle, separated unto the gospel of God."*

The Greek word that is translated "servant" is *doulos.* No translator apparently has been satisfied with the translation "a servant" or "a household slave." The reason is that the Holy Spirit has given it another meaning. It reads like this: "The little love slave of Jesus Christ."

The name "Paul" means "the little one," so "a love slave" is Paul's most endearing title. He has become a slave to this new kind of love.

Sons and servants cannot always be trusted, but a love slave can be trusted to the very limit. The challenge comes to us to become love slaves of Jesus Christ.

This new kind of love has captured us and enslaved us, until we cry out, "Oh, Master, accept me, enroll me as a slave of this new kind of love. There is no sacrifice too great, no place too hard. Love impels me and is driving me to be one with You in this ministry for a lost world."

CONSTRAINING LOVE

There is a master thought in 2 Corinthians 5:14: *"For the love of Christ constraineth us."* Weymouth translates it, *"For the love of Christ overmasters us"* (WEY).

Someone had accused Paul of being beside himself. He explains it on the ground that this new kind of love has overwhelmed him and gained the ascendency in his life.

Moffatt's translation puts it this way:

For I am controlled by the love of Christ, convinced that as One has died for all, then all have died, and that he died for all in order to have the living live no longer for themselves but for him who died and rose for them. (2 Corinthians 5:14–15 MOFF)

When we learn the secret of this strange, new kind of love, it will gain the mastery over us as it did with Paul. It will make us lovers like God. There will no longer be any fear of man, for this love will cast out all that demoniacal fear. On the one hand, it will make us as gentle as Jesus; on the other hand, it will make us conquerors.

We understand what it means to have love abounding in all its fullness through us. It will illumine the knowledge we have gained from our study of the Word.

And this I pray, that your love may abound yet more and more in knowledge and all discernment. (Philippians 1:9)

Above all things being fervent in your love among yourselves. (1 Peter 4:8)

The word *fervent* means "white-heated" or "heated to the welding point." When love becomes white-heated, the whole congregation will blend into one.

The blacksmith heats the metal until it is white-heated. Then he puts the two pieces together, and they became welded together as one. Welded together in love! Wouldn't that make a beautiful church, fitly framed and welded together, made after the design of the Father Himself?

You remember the Father gave Moses the design of the tabernacle and the holy of holies. Now He has designed the church, and He is going to weld it together into one, so that we may be one even as He and the Father are one. (See John 17:21.)

The church can only be welded together with this Jesus kind of love.

> *That their hearts may be comforted, they being knit together in love, and unto all riches of the full assurance of understanding, that they may know the mystery of God, even Christ.*
>
> (Colossians 2:2)

Do you see the wealth wrapped up in this? Hearts knit together in love. As love touches the mind and illuminates the spirit, the fullness of assurance fills your very being.

How we have prayed for faith and power, but this eliminates all that useless struggling. We have the fullness and ability of God; the very sufficiency of God is in us.

BEING ESTABLISHED IN LOVE

> *Now may our God and Father himself, and our Lord Jesus, direct our way unto you: and the Lord make you to increase and abound in love one toward another, and toward all men, even as we also do toward you; to the end he may establish your hearts unblamable in holiness before our God and Father, at the coming of our Lord Jesus with all his saints.*
>
> (1 Thessalonians 3:11–13)

Can you conceive of anything more beautiful than these words? The evangel must be set on fire with love. A loveless church is no evangel. The Father wants us to love one another and to love all men, that being the objective to the end that we may be established in our hearts at the coming of the Lord Jesus.

Increasing in love is like increasing in physical strength or knowledge. This would imply that our ability to absorb, reveal, and give love is unlimited.

Love is the one thing in the human that never grows old, never wears out. It is something as imperishable as the human spirit, something so much a part of the Father that when we and the Father become united and utterly one, we pass out of the failure realm into the realm of the resurrected Christ.

To sense knowledge, the cross appeared to be a failure, but in reality, it was leading to the resurrection, where victory crowned the Christ, not with thorns but with a diadem of love.

They crowned the weak and helpless Christ with thorns. God crowned the resurrected Christ with a crown of glory. That crown is made up of the love of the multitudes whom He has redeemed.

Love will make you what your heart has craved. If you follow the law of love, you cannot fail!

7

GOD-INSIDE MINDED

And we know and have believed the love which God hath in us.
God is love; and he that abideth in love abideth in God,
and God abideth in him.
—1 John 4:16

We have come to know the love way is best. We have come to believe in love. We believe it is better than force, better than argument, better than money, and better than going to court.

The hardest thing for some of us to learn is that the love way is best, that we cannot fail if we walk in love.

It has been hard for us to believe in God's love for us when difficulties came into our lives, but we know now that all of these abnormal things are not the product of love. They come from the adversary, who is seeking to dethrone love in our hearts.

For us to become God-inside minded is for us to become victors. As soon as we become conscious of God inside us, we will begin to depend upon the God inside. We will know that *"greater is he that is in you than he that is in the world"* (1 John 4:4).

There will be a holy boldness in us, a Jesus-like fearlessness. No matter what happens to us, He is inside, and He will take us over. We have His ability, His courage, and His strength. It takes us out of the failure realm and puts us over into the realm of success.

For if, through the transgression of the one individual, Death made use of the one individual to seize the sovereignty, all the more shall those who receive God's overflowing grace and gift of righteousness reign as kings in Life through the one individual, Jesus Christ.   (Romans 5:17 wey)

We have received the gift of righteousness. We have received the abundance of grace. We reign as kings in the realm of life and love. God never intended that we should be servants or have a servile spirit. Love takes us out of the servant realm up into the Son realm.

Love takes the sense of inferiority away from us and gives us the sense of our oneness with Christ. The old inferiority complex that comes from sin consciousness has been destroyed. Love consciousness and Son consciousness have taken its place.

One cannot have a servile spirit and enjoy the reality of sonship. We are masters, we are conquerors, and we are overcomers because we are one with Him. We have His ability, His wisdom, His strength, and His love.

Spiritually, we are free men. We abide in God, and God abides in us.

LOVE AND WISDOM

Wisdom is the ability to use knowledge. It matters not how much knowledge we have; if we haven't wisdom to use it, we will be failures. That is the reason why a large percentage of the men and women who graduate from our colleges and universities make a failure of life. They have knowledge, but they lack wisdom.

First Corinthians 1:30 tells us, *"But of him are ye in Christ Jesus, who was made unto us wisdom from God."* God is love. If we walk in love, we will walk in wisdom.

When love governs our life, we will say nothing that injures anyone.

You remember that statement in Proverbs 6:2: *"Thou art snared with the words of thy mouth."*

We would never have signed that paper had love governed us. We would never have entered into that contract if love had governed us. We might not have married as we did if love had been our master. If we had yielded to love and let it have dominion over us, the mistakes that have marred our lives would never have taken place.

Love, in the final analysis, is wisdom. It has caused us to create, invent, and search until we have discovered things that will make others happy.

Love will make us thoughtful, gentle, and tender. When we speak, there will be something in our voices that will win people to us. We will not only be in earnest, but we will speak wisdom in love.

When we love people, it is easy to work for them.

If you are a preacher and want to be a success, love will be the key that opens the door to success. People will want you because you are a lover. They will come to hear you because everyone wishes to hear a lover. They will linger to talk with you because they want to be loved.

So the Master tells us, *"abide ye in my love"* (John 15:9).

LOVE HUNGER

Everything that has life longs for love. In my ministry, I found that the whole world was love hungry. They put up with their old, selfish, human love for the want of something better. But oh, how they respond to the Jesus kind of love!

Boys and girls are love hungry. They go to the arms of love with utmost freedom. If you want to reach them, love them. Never scold. Don't criticize. Don't tell them how bad they are; tell them how good they may be. Never preach sin; preach its cure.

Tell men and women that God so loved them that He gave His Son for them. Tell them the story of love's unveiling, and you will win their hearts.

When they ask for bread, don't give them a stone. Give them the Bread of Life.

Don't give them your philosophy about love. Unveil Jesus to them.

8

SEEING MEN THROUGH LOVE'S EYES

We have been seeing men through sense-dominated eyes. Now we see them as the Father sees them. I am sure He saw them through the eyes of faith. It was love, seeing men through the eyes of faith.

He believes they will respond to the sacrifice made in Christ. He believes they will want eternal life that will give them joy where sorrow has reigned, victory when failure has held carnival.

He believes men will respond to His love and will come over into the love way. He can see the sinner as a recreated man. He sees the believer as a victor. He sees him walking in love.

We must close our natural sense-ruled eyes and see others as the Father sees them, through the eyes of our heart. He sees the poor made rich, the naked clothed, and selfishness turned into love.

Our faith must arise to meet His faith. Then we can help others. But as long as we see them through sense-governed eyes, we will never be able to take Jesus's place and do the love acts that Jesus did.

The new creation must become love conscious. It is love that is going to lead us out of the labyrinth of selfishness in which we have been walking and struggling all these years. It is love that will put us over and make us winners in life's fight.

We have been need conscious. And as long as we are weakness conscious and sickness conscious, faith will have no place in our lives. But when we yield ourselves to the lordship of love and cut every shore line that binds us to selfishness, love will put us over and make us conscious of what we are.

You remember that striking sentence in Ephesians 2:10, "*We are his workmanship, created in Christ Jesus.*" That means we are God's workmanship, just as creation was His workmanship.

This new creation is His workmanship, and just as the first creation was perfect, we believe this new creation is perfect. The first creation pleased Him, and we know this one does.

He is the Lover. He created us in love. He has built love into us. He has taken the things of Jesus, the things of love, and built them into us. As we act on the Word, it becomes built into us and forms a part of us.

He did not make us to be slaves of circumstances or demons. He did not create us in Christ Jesus to be servants of world influences, but He created us in His Son that we might reign with Him now as victors in the realm of life.

He planned that we should walk in love and act in His stead. We actually take His place.

It is beautiful that we can be so united with Him, so utterly one with Him, that His life absorbs and takes us over—He living in us and loving through us both in word and in deed.

The word translated *power* in Acts 1:8 is *dunamis*, which in a true translation should read "ability." Jesus said He wanted the disciples to tarry in Jerusalem until they received power from on high. That power was love. Only love could conquer the Roman Empire and the Jewish Sanhedrin that had crucified Jesus.

When you receive love, you are receiving the ability of God. You are clothed from on high with God's ability.

Something new has come to man. Failure and the sense of inferiority that had become a part of the consciousness of man has been overthrown.

Now unto him that is able to do exceeding abundantly above all that we ask or think, according to the power that worketh in us.

(Ephesians 3:20)

Love is able to do exceeding abundantly above all that we could ask or even think. It is according to the ability of love that is functioning in us. We are going to surrender our weakness to that love. We are going to let love's ability make us a success.

The old curse of inferiority complex that has held men in bondage since Adam sinned in Eden at last has found its master.

Love in us is greater than anything that can oppose us. Love has made us conquerors today.

Love has led us out of the wilderness of doubts and fears into the rose-strewn fields of God's grace and omnipotence.

At last, we have won! At last, we are conquerors!

9

TAKING OUR PLACE IN LOVE

A home could never be destroyed if every member could be taught to take his place in love.

The wife would never remember the past mistakes of her husband, nor the husband ever remind the wife of any unpleasant happenings. All the mistakes and failures of the past would be wiped out.

What homes we would have! There would be no more quarreling over finances and no more bitter words. Each one would be walking in love.

Love never takes advantage of anyone. Love always bears the burdens of the weak. Love says, "It is all my fault, dear. Had I done differently, or spoken differently, or lived in love, it would never have happened."

There never has been a divorce in a home where the husband and wife both walked in love. This is the solution of the divorce problem.

When men and women receive eternal life, the nature of the Father God, and let that nature dominate them, they grow in this new kind of love until eventually it absorbs them, takes them over, and renews their minds until their thinking is in the realm of love. All suspicion and jealousy die out because there is no soil for them to take root.

The men and women who walk in this new kind of love never injure anyone, never take advantage of anyone. They simply walk and live in God.

No matter what evil the adversary may bring into a life, love will change that evil so that it will bring forth good fruit.

You remember that Jesus said, *"All things are possible to him that believeth"* (Mark 9:23). That means "a believing one" or "a child of God."

You can understand it now. The believing one is linked up with God. He is a branch of the vine. The branch is the fruit-bearing portion of the vine.

He has a legal right to the Father's love and Jesus's ability. He has a legal right to use Jesus's name, which has all authority behind it. He really has the power of attorney to use that name.

The real lover is taking Jesus's place in life. He is a reproduction of Jesus. He is carrying out the dreams and will of the Father as Jesus did.

You remember He said, *"I am come down from heaven, not to do mine own will, but the will of him that sent me"* (John 6:38). Jesus was the first man who ever walked in love.

When selfishness is eliminated in us and love gains the ascendency, we will not seek our own any longer. We will live as the Master lived in His earth walk. We will seek only the Father's will, which will be for the best interests of all the Father's children.

If we walk in love, we will be walking as Jesus walked. We will give ourselves for the redemption of the world, just as Jesus gave Himself. We cannot die for their sins, but we can live the love life for their salvation. We will slowly but surely develop into real lovers like our Lord.

Faith will no longer be a struggle or a thing to be desired.

LOVE'S CHALLENGE

Love is challenging the lovers to come into a richer, more beautiful Christian experience, to leave the lowlands of doubt and fear and enter into their inheritance.

> *Giving thanks to the Father who did make us meet [able] for the participation of the inheritance of the saints in the light.*
>
> (Colossians 1:12 YLT)

God is our ability. He is able to make your life a success.

There isn't a thing in the new covenant or in the finished work of Christ that does not belong to you. He is able to make you all that His great heart desires you to be.

He delivered you out of the hand of the enemy. He gave you His own nature. He made you a new creation. You are His workmanship, created in Christ Jesus. (See Ephesians 2:10.)

He is in you now, living and working His own good pleasure. You are to yield to His Word and His sway and let Him have the right of way in you.

You have written yourself up as a failure for the last time. From today, you step into the new ranks of the conquerors, the overcomers, and the people who put things over. You can do all things in Him, who is your strength, your wisdom, and your ability.

Let the world hear you confess what God's ability is in you. They have heard your confession of weakness and failure. Now change your song and sing the song of a victor.

Every time you confess weakness, you become weaker. Every time you tell people about your sickness, you grow worse. Every time you tell people about your lack, you have more lack.

Begin to confess your fullness and the ability of God to make good. Tell the world that you are more than a conqueror and that you have no other testimony to give.

It thrilled me through and through the first time I ever said the words, "Christ now lives in me."

I had expected Him to be with me, but I was not quite sure but that I would leave Him sometime. I was afraid that sometimes He would forget to go along. Then it came into my spirit consciousness that He was in me, and greater was He that was in me than he that was in the world. (See 1 John 4:4.)

Christ was in me! What couldn't I do? I could get an education. I could develop latent abilities. I could become a blessing to the world. Why? Because He was in me. His enabling ability was there.

Feverishly, I scanned the pages of Paul's epistles to get the proof of this mighty fact that I had God in me, that God was at work within me, willing and working "*for his good pleasure*" (Philippians 2:13).

I knew that I was no longer in the failure ranks. I knew I had moved into the success realm. I knew God and I were united. He was not on the outside any longer. He was not only with me, but He was in me.

Oh, the wonder of it, the thrill of it, the amazing grace of it— God in me! And the biggest asset of the whole thing was that He loved me!

"*The Son of God, who loved me, and gave himself up for me*" (Galatians 2:20). He had identified Himself with me in my earth walk. There could never be any separation from now on. I would not give Him up, and He would not give me up.

I have His life. He has mine. He gives me His ability.

We labor together, my Lord and me.

10

A MOTHER'S CONFESSION

The mother said, "It is no use, I can't do anything with my girls. Two of them are in high school, and one is in grade school. I have lost control over them. I have scolded, threatened, done everything, but it is of no avail."

I said, "Mother, have you tried love?"

"You know I love them," she said.

"I am not speaking of that kind of love. You came to seek help from me. You wanted advice for your family, and I am going to give it to you. Let me ask you some questions. Do you know anything about the Jesus kind of love?"

Her face was blank as she looked at me. "I don't know what you mean."

I made as clear as possible the fact of the two kinds of love.

"I think I see the reason for my failure," she said. "I have never had anything but mother love. I want this Jesus kind of love."

I explained to her how simple it was to receive it, that it would come to her when she received eternal life.

"How may I receive eternal life?" she asked.

"Do you know that Jesus died for your sins?"

"Yes. I believe He did."

Then I shared Romans 10:9–11 with her:

Because if thou shalt confess with thy mouth Jesus as Lord, and shalt believe in thy heart that God raised him from the dead, thou shalt be saved: for with the heart man believeth unto righteousness; and with the mouth confession is made unto salvation. For the scripture saith, Whosoever believeth on him shall not be put to shame.

Then I asked her if she knew that God raised Jesus from the dead for her justification.

"Yes. I do know that."

"Do you confess Him as your Lord?"

"I do."

"Then according to God's Word, what are you?"

"I am saved."

I explained to her that she had received eternal life, the nature of the Father God, that the Father is love, and she had received into her heart this new kind of love. I urged her to yield to that love, study the Word, and begin to practice love in her home.

Days went by, and she finally came to see me. Her face was aglow.

She said, "One of my girls asked me what had happened to me. I told her I had accepted this Jesus kind of love, and she wanted to know how she might receive it. I told her to read your little tract on 'How to Become a Christian.' She did, and together with her sister, she was born again. They both have found this Jesus kind of love."

WALKING IN LOVE

This is the walk of the recreated spirit, the walk of one who has received the love nature of the Father. To walk in love is actually to live in God.

If ye abide in me, and my words abide in you, ask whatsoever ye will, and it shall be done unto you.   (John 15:7)

In other words, if you live in love and love lives in you, ask and you will receive.

It is the realm where the Word dominates, where faith functions. Faith grows in the atmosphere of love. Faith becomes a dominating and creative force when love really rules.

It is the realm of fellowship with the Father, with the Word, and with one another. The sweetest thing about this love life is fellowship. We come together without suspicion, in utter unselfishness, to give our best. We come to give.

The person who comes to get is impoverished by getting. How many Christian workers have lost the beauty and fragrance of life by always dreaming of getting rather than giving?

As we live in this realm of love, the Holy Spirit is able to guide us into all truth, all reality. (See John 16:13.)

As we walk in love, the Word opens and becomes responsive to us. God is in His Word, and as we read it, our hearts are filled with joy and gladness.

I question if anyone can ever understand the Psalm 23 until they abide in this realm of love.

Repeat the first verse softly: *"The LORD is my shepherd; I shall not want"* (KJV). The Hebrew word for *Lord* is *Jehovah*, which is a word of three tenses—past, present, and future. He is the Jehovah of yesterday and the God of now, and He will be the same tomorrow.

He is our Shepherd, so we do not want. He is leading us into the rich pastures of fellowship, into the marvelous fields of love that we find in the Word.

The Spirit's unveiling of the Word is love's unveiling. He is letting us see Himself in the Word. We see Him as the Father, the Lover, the Comforter, and the Overcoming One.

Walking in love means vast possibilities of growth, development, and entering into our rights and privileges in Christ.

We come to understand the reality of His indwelling. We remember that the greater One is in us, and His ability is at our disposal.

We remember that His Word on our lips has dominating authority. We rule diseases and circumstances as we walk in love. We take Jesus's place, speak Jesus's words, and do Jesus's work.

It leads us into the reality of His ability in the living Word. Some of us have never grasped this, but God's ability to heal the sick is in the Word. It becomes mighty on our lips in prayer.

When we love someone, we act on their word unconsciously.

We love Him, and we act on His Word unconsciously.

It is no effort to believe. Love never tries to believe, never tries to have faith. The very word *love* suggests faith. Love makes our faith become limitless.

Now we can understand, as never before, our utter oneness with Him. This blessed oneness suggests our usefulness and our ability to help men.

WE ARE IN GOD'S CLASS

God is a spirit. We are spirits. God has imparted His nature to us. His nature is love. It is the most normal thing for us to live, talk, and act love. Our greatest difficulty has been that we forget what we are in Christ. We remember what we have been. We remember what we were in the old life. We remember our failures, our weaknesses, and our lack, but we forget that the new creation is the end of failure because God has imparted Himself to us.

We remember that Paul said, "*I can do all things in him that strengtheneth me*" (Philippians 4:13). There is no lack, no weakness, and no problem that He cannot solve. There is no difficulty that He cannot surmount, no disease that He cannot heal.

He is in us. His ability is ours. His grace is ours. His love is ours. We have become one with Him.

11

SELFISHNESS IS ABSORBED IN LOVE

Love is God's crucible, God's melting pot, where He melts us all into one.

We become one with Him. That union is love. It is the solution of all the problems that confront us.

If there were a chair in our universities where a thorough course could be taught on the two kinds of love, it would revolutionize them. It is the most vital thing and the most important thing in the world. Yet we know so little about it.

Natural, human love has become the goddess of the divorce court, the football of lawyers. What fortunes they salvage from the wreckage of human love! If this Jesus kind of love gained the supremacy in our country, it would put a large percentage of lawyers out of business.

The major portion of diseases that put men and women under a doctor's care come from the irritations and nervousness of thwarted, natural human love. When a person becomes jealous, that jealousy poisons the blood in his system and brings on stomach trouble or some other eruption in his body.

The awful plague that followed World War I was caused by hatred that had been developed by the Old World. That hatred had poisoned the system, the bloodstream of the human race, and after a while, it turned into that deadly plague.

It is almost impossible for a man or woman to be healed whose mind and heart are filled with hatred.

Beloved, let us love one another: for love is of God; and every one that loveth is begotten of God, and knoweth God.   (1 John 4:7)

Only lovers know each other. We may live with a man or woman for forty years and not truly know that person. Only love opens the heart and reveals the depth of our nature.

Everyone who loves is born of God. It is God's test that we may know the reality of the Jesus love in us.

Unless we are born of God, we will not love. We may feign love, or we may try to imitate love, but we will not be successful. Love is reality.

Romans 8:9 tells us, *"But if any man hath not the Spirit of Christ, he is none of his."* That does not mean the Holy Spirit. That means the spirit that dominated Jesus's life, just as our spirits dominate us. The Christlike spirit is a love spirit. Jesus was a lover. Jesus loved Zacchaeus, He loved Judas, and He loved Pontius Pilate.

The reason He healed the sick was not to prove that He was God. He could not help it. He loved them, and human suffering challenged Him. He died on the cross because He loved us. He loved us, *"and gave himself up for us"* (Ephesians 5:2).

"Let love be without hypocrisy" (Romans 12:9). In other words, let love be without selfishness because selfishness always breeds hypocrisy.

Selfishness is the outlaw in the realm of love. It breaks into that realm and seeks to dethrone love and take its crown. Selfishness is a bold, wicked robber. It makes men dissemble. It breaks friendships. It wrecks homes. It ruins churches. It destroys the fruit of love.

There is only one force able to conquer selfishness and destroy its effectiveness in the lives of men. That force is the new kind of love.

The natural man loves a woman because she satisfies the desires of his heart. He doesn't think of making her happy. He only desires pleasure for himself. If he cannot have her affections, he would rather destroy her than have another man win her. Love murderers are a part of human history. Through neglect, natural human love turns to hatred, jealousy, and murder.

Only a few months ago, a man standing in the courtroom in one of our coast cities said to the judge, "I loved her so I could not help it. I killed her."

Agape, the Jesus kind of love, never turns to jealousy, bitterness, hatred, or murder. It is the solution of the human problem. There is not a phase of life that it does not meet the issue.

Because of it, the laboring man will do more than he is hired to do, and the employer will pay more than the laborer asks. There will be no quarreling between them. Each will seek to give more than the other gives.

Can't you see what it would mean to the commercial world? There would no longer be this deadly competition of the strong destroying the weak.

When God's nature comes into a man, and he gives that nature sway, he cannot do differently than Jesus would in his place.

In Ephesians 5:2, the Spirit tells us to *"walk in love." Walk* means *conduct.* It means the businessman's attitude toward his competitor or his customer. We are going to treat men as God treats them.

Sense knowledge has kept us in slavery.

Do you understand what I mean by sense knowledge? All the knowledge that man possesses, which is taught in our grade schools, colleges, and technical schools, has come to us through the five senses: seeing, hearing, tasting, smelling, and feeling. Our body has been the laboratory, and all our knowledge has come to us through experimentation.

Sense knowledge cannot understand spiritual things nor spiritual values. Consequently, love has never been given its place. We have used it as a toy, as a means to an end.

Now the hour has come when love must have its place.

Society is going to break under the strain. Anarchy is going to reign.

Do you know what anarchy is? It is selfishness without restraint. It is the absence of God. It is man attempting to solve life's problems and leaving God out of his reckoning. That makes him an anarchist.

12

THE LOVE OF CHRIST CONSTRAINETH

Someone asked, "Why did you go to Africa?"

The answer was given, "Because love drew me, and love drove me there. I could not help it."

The love of Christ becomes the mightiest force in the world to the man who is yielded to it. It constrains us or holds us back from saying or doing what we should not. It may cause us to do or give.

When this Jesus kind of love gains control over a man's spirit and takes possession of his thinking, he unconsciously becomes a Jesus man. He will think in terms of love; he will find that he can no longer do things as he has done them in the past.

If he is a businessman, love will get into every phase of his life. If he is working for a firm, he will find that he must work as Jesus would in his place. He does not take advantage of the company because he is working from the heart. He always gives more than he gets. He keeps the company in debt to him.

If he employs help, he takes the place of the Master and seeks to give instead of get. This new kind of love changes *getting* into *giving*. It destroys the soil out of which selfishness finds its strength.

You see love is revolutionary; it is not commonplace. It changes the crude base metals of the human into the most priceless. It takes a common man and makes him uncommon.

I know a man who has no education, no training, and has always lived in semi-poverty—and yet he is much wanted. How quietly they listen when he speaks! What is it that he offers? It is love. He actually lives the Jesus life.

"IF A MAN LOVES ME"

Jesus never said a more searching thing than this:

If a man love me, he will keep my word: and my Father will love him, and we will come unto him, and make our abode with him. (John 14:23)

He says, "If love rules in you, I will come in and live with you. If love governs your home life, I will feel at home with you."

Can you see what that would mean to us? How it would sanctify the home! How safe that home would be if Jesus and the Father lived in it! What it would mean to the children, growing up in the atmosphere and presence of Jesus and the Father!

The problems of rent, taxes, and bills would be solved. If Jesus lived in the house, He would meet the bills.

We remember when Jesus sat in Peter's boat to talk to the multitudes. Afterward, the Lord told the disciple to put out into the deep and let down his nets for a catch. Peter said, "*Master, we toiled all night, and took nothing: but at thy word I will let down the nets*" (Luke 5:5). And they caught so many fish, it took two boats to hold them all.

Jesus paid for the use of Peter's boat. If He lives with you, He will pay your bills. Not only that, but see what it would mean to have the Father God and Jesus with you. How safe the home would be!

He that hath my commandments, and keepeth them, he it is that loveth me: and he that loveth me shall be loved of my Father, and

I will love him, and will manifest myself unto him.

(John 14:21)

His commandment was that we should love one another, even as He loved us.

He will unveil Himself in the Word. You will come to know Him as intimately through the Word as you know the dearest friend or loved one. He will unveil Himself to you if you love Him. He never unveils Himself to those who do not love Him. He was silent when they stripped Him naked and crowned Him with thorns.

He reveals Himself to the lover.

Even as the Father hath loved me, I also have loved you: abide ye in my love. If ye keep my commandments, ye shall abide in my love; even as I have kept my Father's commandments, and abide in his love. (John 15:9–10)

Can you imagine what it would mean to live in love? It would mean the end of strife, the end of quarreling and bitterness, and living in His love. A husband and wife who live in love would live in a heaven-like atmosphere, wouldn't they?

A LITTLE CHILD SHALL LEAD THEM

Children who grow up in that atmosphere would never know what quarreling and bitterness meant.

A little boy who had grown up in this kind of atmosphere, had never heard his father or mother quarrel, and never had heard a bitter word spoken in their home, went to live for a week with his aunt and uncle while the father and mother took a trip to a distant city.

For the first time in his young life, the boy heard a man swear at his wife. The child listened in amazement and began to cry. His uncle took him in his arms and said, "Danny, what is the matter, dear?"

Between sobs, the little boy said, "Uncle, I thought you loved Auntie."

The uncle said, "I do."

"Oh, no you don't; you don't love like Daddy does, or like Mamma loves. They never say bad words."

The man looked at the child and turned to his wife. "Dear, I guess we have missed a great deal in life, haven't we?" he said.

You see, the man who misses love misses the most beautiful thing that life has to offer.

One day, a little boy whose parents had been listening in to our broadcast said, "Mamma, if we had that Jesus kind of love in our home, we would be happier, wouldn't we?"

The mother told it to the husband that night when he came home. The man said, "You know, I have been thinking about it ever since that address that Sunday morning on 'the Jesus kind of love,' and if you are willing, I am. We will invite the Master to come and live with us. I want that kind of love."

He then told the little boy. The child clapped his hands and said, "Won't we be happy, Daddy?"

You see, children want love. No parent has a right to deny his children this Jesus kind of love. It should be preached from the pulpit until every member of the congregation becomes love conscious, until it would be impossible for them to quarrel or say unkind things to one another.

13

LOVE PERFECTED IN US

Herein is love made perfect with us, that we may have boldness in the day of judgment; because as he is, even so are we in this world. There is no fear in love: but perfect love casteth out fear.
—1 John 4:17–18

That is masterful. As He is now at the right hand of the Father, so are we in our earth walk. Why? Because His nature is in us. The great, mighty Holy Spirit who raised Jesus from the dead is in us. We are united with Him in life, and life is love.

We can understand how love can be perfected in one's life. We may never be perfect in wisdom, may never be perfect in knowledge, but we may have love perfected in us.

What a thrilling fact! Love so fills us that fear has no place in our life. We have the use of the name of Jesus that has all authority over demons, disease, circumstances, and the laws of nature, so the source of fear is vanquished.

Love lifts one out of the commonplace into the supernatural. This revelation of love is given to enable us to face the problems that are bound to confront us in these last days as victors.

The book of Revelation shows us how love finally conquers, how the armies of men and demons are overcome by the Lamb. The Lamb is love. Over twenty times in the book of Revelation, Jesus is called *"the Lamb"*—literally "the baby Lamb" or "the helpless Lamb."

We see how helpless love is, and yet love conquers. Love finally dominates, for *"God is love"* (1 John 4:8).

PERFECT LOVE

The Master said, *"A new commandment I give unto you, that ye love one another; even as I have loved you, that ye also love one another"* (John 13:34). If we love like this, we will never injure anyone, we will never take advantage of anyone, and we will never say anything we ought not to say or do anything we should not do.

He commanded them to love one another under the old law, but they had no ability to do so.

Now He has given us the love nature, and it is easy for us to do the things He commands us to do. It is easy for a child to love its parents because that is natural. This new kind of love has made us natural lovers. We love because He first loved us, and to obey the love law is easy.

The old law was called the law of death (see Romans 8:2) because it had a penalty attached to each of the commandments.

There is no penalty attached to this new covenant law. The only penalty is that we suffer when we step out of the love life. Every step out of love is a step into trouble. If you will think back over your life, you will find that every mistake you have ever made has been when you stepped out of love or acted out of love.

The bitter words you spoke that separated you from someone you loved was a step out of love. Every time we bruise or hurt someone, we step out of love.

THE LOVE LAW

Under the first covenant, there were many rules and regulations. Many laws given to regulate the lives of the old covenant men, but there was no inward ability to do or obey.

In this new covenant, there is only one law and one word: love. That law is to govern man in every phase of his life. We have God's nature in us to enable us to do it.

Love worketh no ill to his neighbor: love therefore is the fulfilment of the law.   (Romans 13:10)

Jesus emphasizes this new law:

Even as the Father hath loved me, I also have loved you: abide ye in my love. If ye keep my commandments, ye shall abide in my love; even as I have kept my Father's commandments, and abide in his love. These things have I spoken unto you, that my joy may be in you, and that your joy may be made full. (John 15:9–11)

Living in love, practicing love in everyday life, will lead one into the joy of the Master, and Jesus's joy will be fulfilled in him. We are to love one another even as He has loved us. When one does this, there is no wrongdoing. No one sins who walks in love. Every step out of love will be a step out of fellowship and joy.

It has taken some of us a long time to believe in love, to believe that love is the solution of every human problem, and that every difficulty could be solved by love.

BELIEVING IN LOVE

And we know and have believed the love which God hath in us. God is love; and he that abideth in love abideth in God, and God abideth in him.   (1 John 4:16)

We do believe in love. We believe in the love that God has in our case. We believe that to walk in love is to walk in the highest spiritual realm. As long as one walks in love, he will never transgress against anyone. We are to walk as sons of God. We are to let God live in us as He lived in Christ.

The person who lives in love lives in God, in God's realm. He is living as God would live in his place. He is letting God unveil Himself in him.

John's first letter sheds more light on this:

Ye are of God, my little children, and have overcome them: because greater is he that is in you than he that is in the world.

(1 John 4:4)

We are born of love. This love of God has come into us, and love in us is greater than any opposition or any enemy that can come against us.

As long as one walks in the realm of love, one has constant fellowship with the Father.

LOVE PREVENTS A MULTITUDE OF SINS

First Peter 4:8 says, *"Above all things being fervent in your love among yourselves; for love covereth a multitude of sins,"* but a better rendering might be, "For love prevents a multitude of sins."

Love not only shields the sinning one from your criticism and your harshness, but it also prevents the quarreling and bitterness that would naturally follow if you had *spoken your mind* as we sometimes do.

I'm sure you have heard the expression, "I gave him what was coming to him. He can't run over me and get away with it." That is not love talking. Love would have suffered in silence. Love would never answer a word.

When they had Jesus on trial, it is said that He *"gave* [Pilate] *no answer, not even to one word"* (Matthew 27:14). That was the Jesus way. That was the love way. They accused Jesus of many things, but He was silent. Love won in the resurrection, didn't it?

Love will win in your case.

THE LOVE OF MANY SHALL WAX COLD

And because iniquity shall be multiplied, the love of the many shall wax cold.   (Matthew 24:12)

This is the only time that the word *agape* is used in the book of Matthew. It is speaking of the apostasy that is coming upon the church; it is going to be an apostasy from love.

Men are going to leave the love realm and go down into the sense realm. They are going to say, "It is no use. We can never walk in love under these conditions. Every man has to fight for himself."

The moment the church leaves the love realm, Satan gains the ascendency. Satan gains the mastery over a man the moment he steps out of love.

NOT SEEKING OUR OWN

Here is the solution of labor and capital. Instead of legislating new laws, we need a revival. Men need to receive this new life. Then they will repeat the words of Paul:

Even as I also please all men in all things, not seeking mine own profit, but the profit of the many, that they may be saved.
                                    (1 Corinthians 10:33)

This is the law that should govern us in our economics. It solves every problem. It straightens out all the rough places in the home life and in church work; each man seeking *"the profit of the many, that they may be saved."*

Paul's ambition was to bring man in contact with Jesus. When he did, and they received the Jesus life and the Jesus love, then they began to walk the Jesus way.

Selfishness is like a great mogul engine drawing the long train of human agony and suffering down through the ages. The unhappy terminal will be the judgment. Let's get off the train. Let's get out of that kind of fellowship. Let's live the love life, live the love way.

It is not preaching; it is loving. It is not criticizing; it is loving. It is not new laws to stop sin and wrongdoing, it is a new kind of life that destroys sin by destroying selfishness.

LOVE'S WAY

Now we that are strong ought to bear the infirmities of the weak,
and not to please ourselves.   (Romans 15:1)

Christ did not please Himself; He gave Himself. So we who are strong give not only our money but we give ourselves. We seek to improve that self and make it a better self.

If we have a voice to sing, we will train it and make it a better voice. Whatever gift has been allotted to us, we hold it as a treasure and develop it and train it to make it a better gift.

His very strength that He has given to us has been to bear the burdens of the weaker ones. His ability that has been given to us is for the benefit of those who lack ability.

There will always be the weak and inefficient. They will be ever learning but never coming to the realities of redemption. Because of this, we must gird ourselves with love to go out and serve the unworthy and selfish, give ourselves as He gave Himself for us.

He did not die for the righteous. He died for the unrighteous. He died for the ungodly. He died for the men and women who have gone wrong, who have nothing to give Him but a shattered life. He takes them over and gives them Himself.

How rich is love in its ministry!

One said of another, "I don't see what she can do for anyone. She has no money. She has no training, no education."

But the other answered, "She has love. Do you know when she laid her hands on that fevered brow, a strange quietness came over the patient. The fever left. The patient looked up with a gentle smile and said, 'I thought it was Jesus touching me.' And the one by her said, 'You are not mistaken.'"

The branch was bearing fruit.

14

WALKING IN LOVE

Walking means daily conduct.

As children of God, walk in love, even as Christ also walked in love toward you. (See Ephesians 5:1–2.) How beautiful life becomes when we walk in love.

Love is God's flower garden of the soul, filled with music and laughter. Kindly deeds, loving looks, little gifts—all of these are a part of the love walk.

When the mother awakens in the morning, she remembers how she loves. She goes about the house, picking up little toys and playthings here and there. She waits for the loved ones who come one by one to gather about the table. She is the queen. Her husband, their father, is the king. The children are the loving subjects of their kingdom.

What a realm! What a place! Never an unkind word is spoken. There are no selfish acts. Each one is living to make the other glad.

The husband carries that atmosphere down to the office. The children carry it to school. The mother lives in it joyously, working and singing the whole day through. The neighbors come in for a little chat. It is hard for them to leave a house of love. They think of their own desolate, loveless homes, and they linger in this sylvan retreat where Jesus lives.

Jesus said, *"If a man love me, he will keep my word: and my Father will love him, and we will come unto him, and make our abode with him"* (John 14:23).

That will be a love home. What a place for babies to be born! What a place for them to play, romp, learn to walk and talk, and take their place in life's great game, in a home where love reigns.

All this is possible. This is not poetry. This is not philosophy. This is the everyday life of the everyday man who walks in love.

Love is the reason for creation's being. Man came on the scene because love wanted him. Love gave him birth. This is a strangely beautiful thing.

Ephesians 3:17 says we are to be *"rooted and grounded in love."* That is so the storms of life will not overcome us.

I saw one going through the deepest sorrow. His home had been torn into shreds spiritually. No cyclone ever left a home in more desperate shape physically than this cyclone left it spiritually.

I watched the wife. She was quiet and calm. No bitter words left her lips. There was no bitterness in her heart. When she spoke to the one who had destroyed all that was beautiful, she told him how she loved him and how sorry she was about it.

I could see that love was waiting for this man who had killed love with wantonness and slain that holy thing. Love was waiting back there, believing in a resurrection. All it required was his footstep to make it arise from the grave.

Love is the only reason for being. Love is the only thing that makes life rich and worthwhile.

But, oh, how ruthlessly love is slain, how unkindly love is starved, how thoughtlessly love is neglected and forgotten.

We thought we would always remember to say the kind words and do the kind deeds on which love feeds. But in the multitude of our activities in life's great fight, we have forgotten so many times.

How we tax love to forgive our forgetfulness, to overlook the thoughtless hurt.

We are to be *"rooted and grounded"* in the very heart of the Master, drawing strength from the very heart of God, enabling us to remember.

That ye may be in strength to comprehend, with all the saints, what [is] the breadth, and length, and depth, and height, to know also the love of the Christ that is exceeding the knowledge, that ye may be filled — to all the fulness of God.

(Ephesians 3:18–19 YLT)

Then He tells us so gently about *"forbearing one another in love; giving diligence to keep the unity of the Spirit"* (Ephesians 4:2–3).

Someone has aptly said, "There are two bears in every home—bear and forbear." I bear for the other, and the other bears for me.

We watch over our words so that we will not do or say anything that would break the tranquility of the atmosphere of love. We speak the truth in love, tenderly, gently.

The words fall from the Jesus man's lips, the Jesus woman's lips. They may be words of correction but they drip with love.

We think in love terms. Out of the heart where love reigns, tender words spring into being. They fill the air around us with the very fragrance and aroma of heaven.

We become tenderhearted and gentle with each other, even as God also in Christ has been gentle and tender toward us.

We live in love. We think in terms of love, and we bless the world.

15

LOVE MINDED

We Christians have a love background. We have a love parentage. We are born of God, and God is love.

We are partakers of His nature, and His nature is love. The new creation is a love creation. It was designed and wrought by love. If love is your nature, selfishness is dethroned.

But we are surrounded by selfishness. Everything connected with the natural life is tinged and colored by selfishness. You see it in the animal creation. You see it in natural man everywhere. Our labor and capital war is the war of selfishness.

The thing that the world needs is the love nature of God, eternal life. We must give this love nature full sway and yield to it absolutely. If you followed the recreated spirit's impulses, you would live just as the Master lived, in love.

But we quench the recreated spirit. We say that we are not able to do it, and that we cannot afford to do it. We are afraid to walk the way of love. We are afraid to depend upon the Word. We are afraid to give love a free course.

We have not taken into consideration that He is with us. He has said, *"Fear thou not, for I am with thee"* (Isaiah 41:10).

Hear Him saying, "Be not dismayed at the great demands that come to you. Give and I will give back to you. For I am your God, and

I am love. Let Me love through you, and I will bless humanity." That is the language of the Holy Spirit to your spirit.

THE FEAR OF MAN SNARES US

We have been afraid, so we have quenched love until it has lost its initiative. It no longer dares to suggest action.

Husbands and wives, do you know there would never be a quarrel in your home if you were big enough to say, "Dear, forgive me. I should not have said that. I should not have done that."

After you have confessed your lack of love and have given love its place, you will stop doing the things that break fellowship and spoil the harmony of your home.

Remember, wife, you are taking Jesus's place in that home. Husband, you are taking the Master's place. Let loose, this love life in you will solve your domestic problems.

I believe that 1 John 4:16 has wrapped up in it the answer to every heart cry and the solution to every problem: *"And we know and have believed the love which God hath in us."* We have believed in love. We have believed that love could not fail.

Everything else has failed. Our human wisdom and our human abilities have failed. We have made life bankrupt because we did not dare to give love its place and let love have the right-of-way.

God is love, and he who loves abides in God, and God abides in him. Now if God is abiding in you, then you have in you the solution to the problem that confronts you if you give Him the right-of-way to solve it.

REASON'S FAILURE

But if you do as Martha did at the grave of Lazarus, you will hinder Him. She said, "Don't roll the stone away. His body is decaying for he has been dead for four days. Had You come earlier, You could have raised him." (See John 11:17–44.)

Human wisdom, born of sense knowledge, gets in the way and mars the plan. It hinders the work of the recreated spirit.

Christ wants to bring deliverance to you, but He wants to bring it in love's way. You want to bring deliverance in reason's way. You cannot do it. You have failed. Your old human love has failed.

Your education and your training have been unable to make you a success. If you will give love its place, things will adjust themselves. You must dare to go the way of love. It will be necessary for you to think of yourself as a lover—to see yourself in your home, in the shop, in the school, or wherever you spend your time in contact with people, as a lover.

Galatians 6:2 says, *"Bear ye one another's burdens, and so fulfil the law of Christ."* You see yourself bearing men and women's burdens. You see yourself acting exactly as Jesus would do in your place.

With love comes the ability to love and do the thing that love would prompt you to do. This love will carry you into the supernatural realm, where you will do the Jesus things. You had been doing mankind's things, which are so dependent upon money, people, influence, and pull. But now, you have changed it all; you have taken the Jesus way.

Sometimes you may feel as though it could not be put over. But you give love the right-of-way and see what happens to you.

Some people say, "If I had money, I would help the poor." That is beautiful, but if you will not help the poor now with what little you have, you would not help them if you were rich. If you cannot share with them now, you would not share with them then. Love shares the half loaf. Love shares the little.

It is seeing yourself now with your limited means, sharing with those who are not as well off as you are. You see yourself ruled by love, giving as Jesus gave.

It is hard to love hypocrites. But Jesus did it, and you can do it too. He loved Judas when he sat at the table, and He knew that Judas had already planned to sell Him for thirty pieces of silver.

He loved the man who drove the nails in His hands.

What Jesus did, you can do, because you have His nature and ability.

16

MAKING LOVE ATTRACTIVE

We should make our gifts beautiful. We should make giving an art and cultivate it until it outshines the arts of those about us.

We should lift it out of duty, out of philanthropy, into the Jesus way and the Jesus reason for giving. We must learn Jesus's technique of giving.

Some people give in such a crude, unlovely way that their gift is repellent. Others have learned the secret of love. They have a beautiful technique. Love puts a fragrance into giving and doing that fills the heart of the receiver with joy.

HOW LOVE GIVES

When love gives, it never pauperizes. Philanthropy pauperizes. Governmental giving is a curse.

The man of the world does not always make the highest order of giver. It is better than not giving, but why can't we, as believers, make giving a beautiful and refined art?

Love will enable us to do it if we meditate on love. We must meditate on love until our words and actions are filled with love, until our looks are in harmony with our words and our deeds.

You can give, but your eyes will condemn. You can speak loving words when the tone in your voice is so sharp and ragged that it tears and wounds.

I have known husbands and wives to give in such a way that they cursed in their giving. They throw it at the person as they would throw a bone to a mangy, ugly dog. They say, "There, take it." Many a child has been cursed in the receiving from its parents.

Some people's giving is like soggy, heavy bread. You must eat it, but you do not enjoy it. There is no need of giving like that. You can give as Jesus gave. But you must put real thought into it. Give it as much thought as you do to your business to put it over.

I know a businessman who had worked night and day to put his business over. Then after success had come, he had to work night and day to keep the thing running. But in those years, he had forgotten to love. He loved the woman he married, but he paid no attention to her. He did not have time. At first, she pitied him, but as years went by, she grew lonely and heart hungry.

Their children were neglected by their father. He gave them plenty of money, scolded them properly, and found fault with them, but he had never put any love into the home end of his business. After he had become a millionaire, this man confessed that his money did not satisfy him because he had no home. He had a magnificent house, sons, and daughters, but he had no love.

There is a home end to your business. Unless you put love there, it will fail and break down.

17

THE MESSAGE OF THE CROSS

The cross was love's method of war on sin.

The cross was love unleashed, let loose, and set free from every anchorage. It was love becoming weak and accepting defeat.

Sin slew the Son, the Son of love, and nailed Him to the cross. That cross was the symbol of Satan's victory, triumphing over God and over love.

Satan had seen Jesus made sin; he had seen God turn His back upon Him. He had witnessed the tragedy of eternity. He had seen the dead Son of love nailed to a cross.

The cross was love's way to the throne. When Jesus said, *"I am the way"* (John 14:6), no one dreamed that the way was the way of a cross. No one can understand it from the Father's point of view.

The Son was made sin. It was the Lamb on a cross. Then the cross was love's way of conquering sin, conquering Satan, and setting man free.

The Lamb of Revelation is the same Lamb who hung on the cross. He conquered sin by love; He conquered the world led by Satan through love.

No one dreamed of the empty tomb and Satan's defeat when they saw Him hanging there on the tree. That cross was the symbol of the defeat and failure of every dream of the men who had walked with Jesus. It was the climax of misery, the very crown of agony. That crown of thorns placed upon the brow of the Master seemed a fitting climax to the tragedy of the ages.

The Man who hung on the cross is yet to be crowned King of the ages. The people who take up their cross—an untrimmed, thorn-covered cross, a brutally heavy cross—may be climbing up their Golgotha because they love Him, because they would rather suffer than run; they would rather endure than fail.

The cross folk are a strange folk; they are the Lamb's folk. They are the folk who will join in His coronation. They can use no carnal weapons; they cannot use reason's method.

Satan always seems to be the victor. We often seem defeated—and yet we are winning all the time. The senses can see only our defeat. Our hearts know we are conquering.

This cross message is a message to us. Jesus said, "If a man loves Me, he will take up his cross and follow Me daily." (See Matthew 16:24.) That is discipleship.

The cross may be heavy and the burden beyond our ability to carry, and yet somehow or other, there is an unseen strength pouring into us.

We bear our cross daily. Our cross does not save us. It is Christ who saves us. We do not bear the cross to make us good; we have the goodness, and that is the reason we bear the cross.

Bearing your cross will lead you into a deeper trust in Him, a finer steadfastness. Your cross may be a person who makes life hell for you, and yet you bear the cross for Jesus's sake.

Your cross may be circumstances that imprison you, and yet in the prison, you crown Him Lord, and you rejoice that you are able to bear the cross within the prison of circumstances.

Your cross may be an unhealed sore in your heart, an old sore, an aggravating grievous sore that memory keeps raw. You bear it. Daily you drink of His grace; daily you feed on the bread of the Mighty One and are strong.

Your cross may be a dead love that you cannot bury. God help you. A dead love that cannot be buried becomes an unseen, unknown cross. It is a hard cross. But there is grace to bear it, and every cross bearer is a winner.

Your cross may be a cherished dream denied. You saw what you could have been, but you stayed by the stuff and let others go. You turned your dream into prayers for others, but you will win.

Just remember that following the cross leads to the empty tomb and the triumphant, resurrected life. Following from the cross and the empty tomb, you go to the coronation. If you have had your cross, you will have your resurrection out of the agony of the cross into the risen life with Jesus Christ.

18

SOME LOVE FACTS

You will need love more as you grow old. Store it up and hoard love so that when the hour of need comes, you will be able to draw on it. Then you will have it.

Real love will destroy all that is unreal. Shame cannot abide in the light of love. Selfishness is destroyed in the heart when love takes over the life.

Self-preservation is the first law of selfishness. The preservation of others is the first law of love.

Only love made it necessary for God to give His Son. Love drove Him to give Jesus. Love drove Jesus to give Himself.

Love is the propelling power that makes us care for the needy and the weak. The strong, according to the love law, must bear the infirmities of the weak and not please themselves.

Selfishness is the mother of practically all of our miseries. Most of our tears are born of selfishness.

Love makes one lighthearted, companionable, and helpful. The Jesus kind of love is God's cure for every ill. Love lifts one out of the realm of the senses into the realm of the spirit.

GOD'S SUPERMEN

The reason love has made supermen of common men is that God is love. When God's nature gains the mastery, one begins to act like God.

It is impossible for the man who has never been recreated to love with this new kind of love. This new love is bound to make the most mediocre person unusual when it becomes the lord of his heart.

Human love is the most beautiful flower that humanity has naturally, but it is a poison flower. It has caused the heartaches, the divorces, the broken homes, and the wrecked families that disgrace our civilization.

The Jesus kind of love has never broken a home. It has never wrecked a life. It has never made a criminal out of a single child. This in itself should awaken thinking men and women.

The moment that one becomes love minded, he becomes broad minded, God minded, and humanity minded. He sees the need. His ears become attuned to catch the sigh and feel the sob of the broken hearts around him.

When we become love minded, we actually take Jesus's place.

The teaching of love in the Gospel of John cannot be understood until one has received the nature of the Father. Jesus said, *"Even as the Father hath loved me, I also have loved you: abide ye in my love"* (John 15:9).

He wants us to live in His love just as you have lived in the love of that man or that woman. He is living in the Father's love, and He wishes us to live in His love.

If we live in love, we begin to bear the fruits of love. The fruit of love will be in the actions, conduct, and words that are born of love. The days of hatred, jealousy, bitterness, and revenge are past.

A NEW ORDER HAS COME

A new day has dawned. It is the love day.

A woman said, "I cannot make you understand the transformation that has come into our home. There was always irritation and friction. This brought out sharp words, sometimes much bitter thought. But since we received eternal life, there has come a tenderness, a beauty of life, and a sweetness of expression that has affected the children as well as my husband and myself. We are living in a love realm.

"The other night, after he had been home a little while from the office, my husband said, 'How beautiful our home has become because each one is making a contribution of love. The children are more thoughtful. They feel the new sweet atmosphere of love, and they respond to it.' Mother is different, daddy is different."

A little boy once said, "Daddy, I wish you would love like Mr. Kenyon told us to over the air this morning. That would make mama and me so happy."

This Jesus kind of love is the answer to the heart cry of childhood, youth, manhood, and old age. It will take the bitterness out of the heart and soften the lines of the face. It will make the husband and wife more than content with their own home.

This love is a home builder and a home preserver. This is God's method of protecting marriage. This is God's method of protecting childhood and motherhood.

When the Jesus kind of love gains the ascendency in the hearts of husband and wife, no other law is necessary to preserve the home.

19

BLOSSOM LIKE THE ROSE

*The wilderness and the dry land shall be glad; and the desert
shall rejoice, and blossom as the rose. It shall blossom
abundantly, and rejoice even with joy and singing.*
—Isaiah 35:1–2

I never knew what this verse meant until recently. It is messianic. It belongs to Christianity.

What is there in Christianity that will make the wilderness and a dry land be glad, and the desert to blossom as a rose? It is the new kind of love that the Master brought to the world. It is the miracle of Christianity.

It is the most amazing feature of the Christ life. It has been the most outstanding challenge to sense knowledge.

The thing about Jesus's life that awakens thought is not His miracles. It is something else. For the want of a better word, we have called it love. But it is not love that can be measured by human love. It was distinctly different.

"*God is love*" (1 John 4:8), and Jesus was God manifested in the flesh. Jesus manifested this love that has gripped the heart of the world. Jesus's attitude toward men and His death on the cross illustrate this new thing.

Every revival of Christianity has been characterized by an outflowing of this love.

The old human love is based upon selfishness. It can easily turn to hatred, jealousy, bitterness, and murder.

But the very provocations that would make the old love turn to bitterness make the new kind of love more beautiful. It *"seeketh not its own"* (1 Corinthians 13:5). It bears with all kinds of persecutions and bitterness; it never sinks to the level of its provocateur.

In these hard days through which the nations are passing, this new kind of love shines out as a beacon, inviting to a higher and better civilization. It lifts us out of the sordid life around us. It keeps us above the strife and bitterness of contending selfishness.

The war among nations is but selfishness coming into full bloom. The war between labor and capital is selfishness gaining the control of the hearts of men, selfishness becoming the master passion that rules the hearts of men.

The Jesus kind of love would eliminate war and destroy selfishness, greed, and the bitterness of classes and the masses. It would solve every economic problem. Where this Jesus kind of love reigns, there would never be a strike.

Where the Jesus kind of love reigns, there would be no more lawsuits. The halls of justice would be turned into meetings of praise and fellowship. Where the Jesus kind of love dominates, divorce never comes.

Jesus brought a new kind of love to the world, fresh from the Father's heart. It cannot be imitated. It beggars a definition by words. Its best definition is Jesus Christ Himself. This new kind of love comes into a barren life and makes it blossom as a rose. It takes away the hardness and bitterness of life.

One day, I was riding through the Mojave Desert with a friend and I said, "How desolate and barren it is." He said, "Yes, but after the first rain, it becomes a paradise of beauty. Those barren hills will be covered with gorgeous flowers."

Then I saw how this love life is. After our first contact with the Master, it makes our desert lives to blossom as a rose. This love can fill the life. There will be no empty lives, no barren lives. Every life may become a garden of delight. God has made it possible.

All that is needed is that Jesus become the Master, the Lord of the life. Then the heart will sing, *"The* LORD *is my shepherd; I shall not want"* (Psalm 23:1 KJV). Love will fill your heart, and there will be songs on your lips. This love will make your barren life a garden of beauty, a thing of joy forever.

20

"GOD IS LOVE"

This title does not mean much unless we know that He is our Father. You say, "God loves me" and note the reaction in your soul. Then you whisper, "The Father Himself loves me," or you say, "My Father loves me now."

You get no sense of nearness from the word *God* but you cannot say the word *Father* without the sense of relationship intruding, pushing itself into your consciousness. So I linger over this precious fact that the Father Himself loves me.

My heart asks, "How much does He love me?" Jesus told us in one of His prayers to the Father *"that the world may know that thou didst send me, and lovedst them, even as thou lovedst me"* (John 17:23). Then the Father loves me *"even as"* He loved Jesus.

I cannot understand it. I cannot reason it out. I take it to my heart and thank Him for it. How utterly beautiful it is, how utterly beyond reason, how out of harmony with everything that I have ever known. It just seems as though we were lifted into a new realm, when He whispers that the Father loves me *"even as"* He loves Jesus.

I feel like a prince, as though I reign in the realm of love, it is so utterly new and wonderful. This Father God is love, and He gives this love nature to us, but we are love's children, children of love.

I cannot take it in. It is too wonderful and yet I hold it to my breast. I shed tears of joy. He loves me. I cannot understand the Father and why He should love me so, but He does.

We reach our best and we do our best in a love atmosphere. Children grow up best in homes of love. Husbands do their best work when love waits for them at home. Wives do their best work when they are expecting love to come home and command it.

Now I can see why every thought, every motive, and every act outside of love dwarfs us, binds us, holds us in bondage, and keeps us from our best. Every love act enriches us. Every love thought makes us better. We think love, then we act love. What a plan it was that planned love for the human!

Love promotes health. God is love; God is my healer. Love is the healer. Now I can understand why bitter thoughts upset the stomach and disturb the circulation of the blood.

I can understand why when a mother is nursing a babe and is filled with anger and bitterness that the milk poisons the child. God never intended that the mother should have anything but thoughts of love while she nurses her child. She should love her husband and everyone around her until her milk is made sweet with her love.

I can understand why every step outside of love is a challenge to disease and failure, unhappiness and weakness. I can understand now that there is only one sin for the believer and that is to step outside of love. All other sins are the children of the mother sin of sins.

If I walk in love, I will never sin. Isn't that wonderful? That solves the problem of human conduct. To live in love's realm and learn love's language, love's methods, and love's way brings about a just education. Now we will whisper again, "God is love, and this love God is my Father; I am His child. I am in love's family.

Jesus is love. Jesus is the way of love where we walk the Jesus way, where we walk the love way. Jesus was love in action, love in manifestation. I will be the same. I will love Him. I will walk with Him. I will introduce Him to the world in my daily life for God, my Father, is love.

LET LOVE WORDS REIGN

Learn to think in terms of love, learn to give in love so that the background of your life, the mother of your actions, is love, this Jesus kind of love. Get love's language; learn it. Let it displace the language of the world.

Sense knowledge has ruled us; now the Jesus kind of love language is to displace it. We are going to learn the little love ways, the gentle, tender beautiful love ways, and how to look love, so our eyes will be love-filled, so men can see Jesus in us. There will never be any more of those little hate acts, selfish acts, or bitter acts or words. All will be tender and beautiful.

We are going to take our words, all of these sense knowledge words, and put them to soak in love. Then when they come forth and leap from our lips, they will have the fragrance of love; they will have the beauty of love, the gentle tenderness of love. There will be something exquisitely beautiful about them.

Wouldn't it be a wonderful thing to have all our words love filled? So many words are hate filled. But we will have just love-filled words.

We will send them out on the air. My voice has been heard over the radio sometimes a thousand or two thousand miles away. One day, a person picked up my voice way over in the state of Maine. It came in as clear as a bell nearly four thousand miles away.

Oh, how important it was that morning that those words should be love filled. They traveled so far through the cold bleak icy weather in the northern part of Maine—warm words, tender words, Jesus-filled words. In order to do this, you must be a Jesus kind of lover who *"seeketh not its own"* (1 Corinthians 13:5) and does not try to rob anyone. Just a lover.

Wouldn't it be beautiful if we could get the love habit, if our conversations could be born out of love, had all the dainty beautiful little tricks of love, the delicate intonation, the sweet beautiful love words blended with love thoughts? Jesus would be manifested in us, wouldn't He?

In our daily walk in our contacts with men and women, it would be love in action. We are Jesus folks. We must live the Jesus life. We must let this love life live in us as it lived in Jesus.

Jesus represented the Father; now we will represent Jesus. We will let love reign as a queen in our homes. How beautiful it will make them.

We are going to let the Jesus kind of love reign as queen in our hearts until every thought that is born there will be born of love, and every thought that is transformed into words will be love thoughts going out through the medium of love words to bless, cheer, comfort, and help.

We are going to let love reign over our reason. We are going to make reason become the servant of love. This may be hard because reason is so self-assertive and so hard to yield, but it must yield to love.

We are going to let Love reign in our businesses until men can feel it in the office. Office help will work better in an atmosphere of love than they do in an atmosphere of hate.

You will get more done in an atmosphere of love. So today, we are going to let love rule us in every way. All we think and do and say will be born of love.

21

WE ARE THE SONS OF LOVE

Christianity is a divine-human love affair. We are born of love. We have received the love nature of God.

This makes Christianity utterly different from every other religion in the world. It is not a religion. It is a love nature imparted to man. It is man rising to the height of this love nature. It is lifting man out of the normal realm in which the human race has been since the fall into the realm of God. It makes us as different from the world as was the Man Jesus.

This has never been clearly taught by the church, yet it is the heart of everything.

Jesus is the head of the new creation. The love law that He gave was to rule it.

> By this shall all men know that ye are my disciples, if ye have love
> one to another.   (John 13:35)

This is the new love commandment, the new love law by which we are to be governed. Jesus is the love Lord. He is the Lord of this new creation.

> A new commandment I give unto you, that ye love one another;
> even as I have loved you, that ye also love one another. By this

shall all men know that ye are my disciples, if ye have love one to another. (John 13:34–35)

This is the badge by which the new creation is known. It is a badge of conduct. It is not like a gold badge worn upon the lapel of a coat, but it is a life. It is acting like Jesus. This is not dogma or creed. This is Jesus in daily life.

Do all things without murmurings and questionings: that ye may become blameless and harmless, children of God without blemish in the midst of a crooked and perverse generation, among whom ye are seen as lights in the world.
(Philippians 2:14–15)

We are blameless and harmless, sons of God. We are lovers, different from other men, because of love at work in our daily lives.

God is love, and God is light.

This is the message which we have heard from [Jesus] and announce unto you, that God is light, and in him is no darkness at all. (1 John 1:5)

If we walk in the fullness of love, we are walking in the light. We have fellowship with the Father. We live in sweetest communion with each other.

I never understood what this Scripture meant:

Ye are of God, my little children, and have overcome them: because greater is he that is in you than he that is in the world.
(1 John 4:4)

This Scripture challenges us. "*Ye are of God.*" You are of love. You have overcome them by love. Greater is the love God in you than the hate god outside.

LOVE'S DOMINION

This strange new relationship with God in us as a lover makes us as gentle and thoughtful as Jesus. Jesus was the gentle love miracle. We have the gentle love miracle in us, loving through us, living in us, reproducing Himself in us.

This life is heaven's light. It is letting Jesus loose in us. It is translating the Jesus life into daily life. It is Jesus set free in us.

It is not a theory, not a creed, not a religion. It is the real Jesus thinking through us, acting through us. It is the love Lord in us unveiling Himself.

Jesus, the lover of old Galilee

Loving and living His life in me,

Meeting men's needs with Jesus deeds.

Yes, Jesus is loving through me.

The great lover is in us now. He is living in us now. "*It is no longer I that live, but Christ liveth in me*" (Galatians 2:20). Jesus is the lover unveiled in a believer.

Greater is the lover in you than any force from without that can touch your life. We can trustfully say, "I am of God." This greater One is He who burst the bars of death asunder and broke Satan's dominion. He is greater than the confusion in your heart or home. He is the absolute monarch of the heart of man.

He is love's dictator, ruling in love in us.

LOVE'S PEACE

"*Peace I leave with you; my peace I give unto you: not as the world giveth, give I unto you*" (John 14:27). His presence in you is your peace and gentle quietness. "*For he is our peace*" (Ephesians 2:14).

How little we have appreciated this. How we have wanted peace and cried for peace, not knowing that peace was in us.

How we have craved for love, not knowing that love was in us.

How we have longed for faith, not knowing that Jesus Christ, who is faith itself, was living in us.

God's peace is greater than the restlessness of the world, the restlessness of your heart and mind. The God of rest is in your heart. He is the God of all quietness.

> *Beloved, let us love one another: for love is of God; and every one*
> *that loveth is begotten of God, and knoweth God. He that loveth*
> *not knoweth not God; for God is love.*   (1 John 4:7–8)

He is the lover, and the lover is in you. He loved in the throes of death upon the cross. He loved when He arose from the dead. He loves now.

"And my God shall supply every need of yours" (Philippians 4:19). Love is greater than your needs. He is the greater One, the Lord of finances, and the Lord of grace. We can rise above home influence, business influence, or any other hindrance because the enabling One is in us.

No matter how unkind men may be, you love them. He loved. You love. He died for them. You live for them. He is in you, the lover of men, loving through you.

THE WINNING POWER OF LOVE

It is giving love its place in life. Love must be first. The believer moves in love. It is the center of his being.

> *Above all things being fervent in your love among yourselves; for*
> *love covereth a multitude of sins.*   (1 Peter 4:8)

It is not passive love. It is a white-heated love. It is not love governed by sense knowledge but love without restraint.

It is love that prevents a multitude of sins. It lifts a man into a realm where he does not quarrel, is not bitter, and does not answer back. It is a white-heated love like the love of the Master.

Love has all the earmarks of Jesus. It is a love that covers up the failings and weaknesses of those about it. It never talks unkindly, never bears a tale. It is the unfeigned love that loves from the heart fervently—a love that lifts us out of the commonplace into its own realm.

This new kind of love is the miracle of the ages. It is love that works within us.

For God it is who is working in you both to will and to work for His good pleasure.   (Philippians 2:13 YLT)

22

THE LOVE LAW INTERPRETED

The book of Leviticus is the interpretation of the Ten Commandments.

This love chapter is the interpretation of the new commandment of the new creation.

> *A new commandment I give unto you, that ye love one another; even as I have loved you, that ye also love one another. By this shall all men know that ye are my disciples, if ye have love one to another.* (John 13:34–35)

> *If I speak with the tongues of men and of angels, but have not love, I am become sounding brass, or a clanging cymbal. And if I have the gift of prophecy, and know all mysteries and all knowledge; and if I have all faith, so as to remove mountains, but have not love, I am nothing.* (1 Corinthians 13:1–2)

The ability to master many languages has been a coveted achievement in the scholastic world, but the Spirit shows us here that one might speak in all the languages of men and angels, yet if he does not have this new kind of love, he is but sounding brass and a clanging cymbal.

Again he says, "*If I have the gift of prophecy, and know all mysteries and all knowledge; and if I have all faith, so as to remove mountains, but have not love, I am nothing.*"

If I have the gift of prophecy so that I could foretell the events of a century, or understand all mysteries and have all knowledge, but have not love, I am nothing.

We all know the struggle of our chemists and metallurgists to unravel the mysteries of the chemicals, metals, and oils of the earth. One may know all these things and beside that, have faith so as to remove mountains, faith like the Master had in His earth walk; he may have all this, but if he does not have the Jesus kind of love, he is nothing.

He takes another step: "*And if I bestow all my goods to feed the poor, and if I give my body to be burned, but have not love, it profiteth me nothing*" (1 Corinthians 13:3).

I may be able to give as Rockefeller or Carnegie, or go into the jungles of Africa and pour my life out in the service of humanity, but if I do not have this Jesus kind of love, my philanthropy means nothing.

> *Love suffereth long, and is kind; love envieth not; love vaunteth not itself, is not puffed up, doth not behave itself unseemly, seeketh not its own, is not provoked, taketh not account of evil; rejoiceth not in unrighteousness, but rejoiceth with the truth; beareth all things, believeth all things, hopeth all things, endureth all things. Love never faileth.*   (1 Corinthians 13:4–8)

We cannot refrain from comparing it with *phileo*—natural, human love. *Phileo* may suffer long but while it suffers, it is bitter, unhappy under the stress. Natural, human love is born of selfishness, and when that selfishness is thwarted, it becomes miserable.

"*Love envieth not.*" The entire economic and social upheaval that is manifested throughout the whole world is caused by the poor envying the rich, and the failures envying the successful. Sense knowledge makes the poor restless, but gives no formula to relieve their condition.

"*Love vaunteth not itself, is not puffed up.*" Natural love does vaunt itself and parade itself; it is ever boasting of its achievements. The Jesus kind of love is the very opposite.

"*Doth not behave itself unseemly.*" Go to the divorce court and note the behavior of natural love. Husband and wife are uncovering the secrets of their past love. Now filled with bitterness, selfishness, and hatred, they war against each other.

Go into the modern home and witness the unhappy condition, how the husband and wife quarrel before the children. How unseemly natural love acts under provocation.

"*Seeketh not its own.*" Selfishness is eliminated. Bible scholar Benjamin Wilson put it this way: "Seeks not what belongs to another." That is striking.

This new kind of love does not seek its own in the divorce court or in the court of law.

What a heavenly thing this new kind of love really is!

"*Is not provoked, taketh not account of evil.*" That would end the reign of scandal. It would eliminate the unhappy suspicion that separates lovers and wrecks homes.

"*Rejoiceth not in unrighteousness, but rejoiceth with the truth.*" It finds no pleasure in sin, no pleasure in wrong, no pleasure in the thing that injures another. Its joy is in the truth.

"*Beareth all things.*" It never repeats scandal. It never remembers the unkindness of the past. Natural, human love remembers the old sins and has the scars on exhibition.

What God forgives, He forgets. This new kind of love is of God. What it forgives, it forgets. It has no memory of old sins.

"*Believeth all things.*" This is a new unveiling of faith. We believe in the person we love. It is hard for us to doubt where love has found a nesting place. Here is the secret of faith. If you want the kind of faith that Jesus had, this new kind of love alone will give birth to it.

"*Hopeth all things.*" This means that under the most adverse circumstances, hope, which is the kindred of joy, holds forth and brings the sense of victory in the presence of defeat.

"*Endureth all things.*" This is perhaps one of the most amazing features of this new kind of love. Through years of suffering and privation, it remains steadfast, immovable, and always abounding in good works. It endures years of self-denial without complaint. This lifts man into the realm of God. This is an unveiling of what God can do in common men.

The next step is the most suggestive perhaps of the entire chapter: "*Love never faileth.*"

Knowledge will break down. Everything else will fail. We have tried force. We have tried law. We have tried willpower. But they have all failed.

The mother has scolded and prayed. She has gone through a miniature hell and has failed. Now she sees a vision. She understands what the Spirit meant in 1 John 4:16: "*And we know and have believed the love which God hath in us. God is love; and he that abideth in love abideth in God, and God abideth in him.*"

It will be a victorious hour when we learn to believe in love. It is something that lifts us into a realm above the senses where we trust in an unseen force.

"*He that abideth in love abideth in God, and God abideth in him.*"

If you trust in love, you trust in God. You can say, "Greater is love in me than this problem that confronts me, this difficulty that has held me in bondage." Love lifts us into the realm of God.

We can understand now why love cannot fail.

FOLLOW AFTER LOVE

We have followed after money, after pleasure, and after the things of the senses.

In 1 Corinthians 14:1, the Spirit says to us, at the close of that marvelous exposition of *agape* in chapter 13, that we are to "*follow after love.*"

God is love. So then it is following after God. We will go where love leads. We will do what love suggests. That is the way Jesus lived. He followed after love.

That was the way Paul walked. He followed after love. Many another voices called and many another roads beckoned, but his path was love.

Jesus's path lead Him to Calvary. Your path may have a Calvary conclusion too.

We set aside the things that we once craved for love's sake, for we are going down the path of love. It may be thorn-filled, or it may be strewn with roses, but we will follow after love.

If it is service in a foreign field, we will follow after love. If love beckons us to go to the slums of our city, we will follow after love.

We know no other path. We know no other way than the love way, the Jesus way.

We can hear Him whisper, "You who are strong ought to bear the infirmities of the weak and not to please yourselves." (See Romans 15:1.)

Christ pleased not Himself. He is your life pattern.

CONCLUSION

There is a love that can stand the test of modern life.

There is a love that will enable us to love the unlovely, the disagreeable, and the hateful.

There is a love that will lift us up into God's class, where we love the ungodly and the unworthy.

There is a love that will make us just like the Master so that we would not only live for men, but also die for them.

There is a love that will enable us to love them when they are doing all they can to injure us.

There is a love that will whisper, *"Forgive them; for they know not what they do"* (Luke 23:34).

Yes, there is a love. If you are a new creation, you have found this new kind of love.

HOW IT WORKS

Yes, this new kind of love works. It can be trusted to do the thing we declare it will do.

It is God's nature gaining the mastery in our lives, and wherever it gains the mastery, it works.

It makes hard, bitter men gentle as Jesus. It will take a man like Saul of Tarsus and make him like Paul. It will take men out of the lowest depths of the slums and lead them into the pulpits, where they will lead multitudes to Christ.

It is the miracle of modern days.

HEED THE CALL

You have read. You have been thrilled. You have been convicted. He, the Unseen One, has been talking to your heart. What are you going to do about it?

You must not ignore the call. This is your great moment. You must respond to the tug of your spirit. Your spirit is craving this deep, rich, wonderful life.

Do not follow sense knowledge. Give your spirit the right of way. Let this love exercise its lordship from this hour. It will make life big to you. It will make you a blessing to the world.

The broken lives and the crushed hearts beating to the rhythm of misery are a challenge. We are attempting to answer that challenge.

We believe we have the message for this crisis hour of human suffering.

God has been speaking to your heart. You have seen the failure of natural human love.

You see what this new kind of love can do for men and women. You know of many homes where they need this message. It would save the home. It would save the children.

Here is the challenge to you: will you stir yourself to send for a few copies to mail to your friends with a letter telling them what this message has meant to you?

Will you see that every clergyman in your city has a copy?

You may do another thing: call in your friends and read the book together with them.

Watch the reactions. You will be filled with joy at this ministry in which you are able to have a share.

It is in your hands now. Don't let the impulse of the Spirit die without action.

ABOUT THE AUTHOR

D_r. E. W. Kenyon (1867–1948) was born in Saratoga County, New York. At age nineteen, he preached his first sermon. He pastored several churches in New England and founded the Bethel Bible Institute in Spencer, Massachusetts. This school later became the Providence Bible Institute when it was relocated to Providence, Rhode Island.

Kenyon served as an evangelist for over twenty years. In 1931, he became a pioneer in Christian radio on the Pacific Coast with his show *Kenyon's Church of the Air,* for which he earned the moniker "The Faith Builder." He also began the New Covenant Baptist Church in Seattle.

In addition to his pastoral and radio ministries, Kenyon wrote extensively. Among his books are the Bible courses *The Bible in the Light of Our Redemption: From Genesis Through Revelation* and *Studies in the Deeper Life: A Scriptural Study of Great Christian Truths,* and more than twenty other works, including *What We Are in Christ, Two Kinds of Faith, In His Presence: The Secret of Prayer, The Blood Covenant, The Hidden Man, Jesus the Healer, New Creation Realities,* and *Two Kinds of Righteousness.*

His words and works live on through Kenyon's Gospel Publishing Society. Please visit www.kenyons.org for more information.

Welcome to Our House!

We Have a Special Gift for You ...

It is our privilege and pleasure to share in your love of Christian classics by publishing books that enrich your life and encourage your faith.

To show our appreciation, we invite you to sign up to receive a specially selected **Reader Appreciation Gift**, with our compliments. Just go to the Web address at the bottom of this page.

God bless you as you seek a deeper walk with Him!

whpub.me/classicthx

WHITAKER
HOUSE